J 508.2 Her
Herrington, Lisa M. author.
How do you know it's winter? /

34028084831818
**TOM** $5.95    ocn841198214
04/15/14

**R**ookie
**Read-About®**
**Science**

# How Do You Know
# It's Winter?

### by Lisa M. Herrington

### Content Consultant
Randy C. Bilik, M.A.
Julia A. Stark Elementary School, Stamford, Connecticut

### Reading Consultant
Jeanne M. Clidas, Ph.D.
Reading Specialist

**Children's Press®**
An Imprint of Scholastic Inc.
New York Toronto London Auckland Sydney
Mexico City New Delhi Hong Kong
Danbury, Connecticut

Library of Congress Cataloging-in-Publication Data
Herrington, Lisa M., author.
  How do you know it's winter? / by Lisa M. Herrington.
    pages cm. — (Rookie read-about science)
  Summary: "Introduces the reader to the winter season."— Provided by publisher.
  Audience: 3-6.
  Includes index.
  ISBN 978-0-531-29949-4 (library binding) — ISBN 978-0-531-22578-3 (pbk.)
  1. Winter—Juvenile literature.  I. Title. II. Title: How do you know it is winter?
III. Series: Rookie read-about science.
  QB637.8.H474 2014
  508.2—dc23                                        2013014929

No part of this publication may be reproduced in whole or in part, or stored in a
retrieval system, or transmitted in any form or by any means, electronic, mechanical,
photocopying, recording, or otherwise, without written permission of the publisher.
For information regarding permission, write to Scholastic Inc., Attention: Permissions
Department, 557 Broadway, New York, NY 10012.

Produced by Spooky Cheetah Press

© 2014 by Scholastic Inc.

All rights reserved. Published in 2014 by Children's Press, an imprint of Scholastic Inc.

Printed in China 62

SCHOLASTIC, CHILDREN'S PRESS, ROOKIE READ-ABOUT®, and associated logos are
trademarks and/or registered trademarks of Scholastic Inc.

1 2 3 4 5 6 7 8 9 10 R 23 22 21 20 19 18 17 16 15 14

Photographs © 2014: Adam Chinitz: 30; Alamy Images/Bill Brooks: 7; Getty Images/
nycshooter/Vetta: cover; iStockphoto: 20; Media Bakery: 24 (Blend Images), 12,
31 center top (Per-Eric Berglund/Stockbyte), 4; PhotoEdit/Richard Hutchings: 27;
Shutterstock, Inc./Jaroslaw Grudzinski: 8; Superstock, Inc.: 16, 29 (Elena Elisseeva/
SuperFusion), 31 center bottom (Juniors), 19, 31 top (NHPA); The Image Works/Aristide
Economopoulos/The Star Ledger: 23; Thinkstock: 28 (Creatas Images/Getty Images),
3 top (Hemera), 3 bottom, 15 (iStockphoto), 11, 31 bottom (Monkey Business).

# Table of Contents

# Welcome, Winter!

The wind howls. Snow covers the ground. Trees lose their leaves. That is how we know it is winter.

These kids are catching snowflakes on their tongues.

These photos show a tree in all four seasons.

There are four seasons in each year. Each season lasts about three months. Winter is the season that comes after fall.

FUN FACT!

The first day of winter is usually December 21$^{st}$ or 22$^{nd}$.

Winter

Spring

Summer

Fall

# What's the Weather?

*Brrr!* Winter is the coldest season. In winter, days are shorter than at any other time of year. That means it gets dark early in the evening.

## FUN FACT!

The first day of winter has the fewest hours of daylight all year.

**Frost** forms on windows. The ice makes patterns. They look like swirls and feathers.

To make frost yourself, try the experiment on page 30.

Time to bundle up! It is cold out there. A coat, mittens, a hat, a scarf, and boots will help keep you warm.

This girl is dressed just right for playing outside in the snow.

15

# Plants and Animals in Winter

Winter brings changes for plants and animals. Most plants stop growing. Leaves have fallen off most trees.

Unlike other trees, evergreens do not lose their needles in winter.

Bears **hibernate** during winter. Chipmunks and mice stay cozy in their underground nests. Some rabbits grow thick fur to stay warm.

This rabbit's white fur acts as **camouflage** in the snow.

# Kids in Winter

In some places, plows clear snow from the streets. Kids help shovel snow from sidewalks and driveways.

This girl is helping her uncle clear their sidewalk and driveway.

Winter sports are fun. We ice-skate, sled, and ski. We also go ice fishing.

## FUN FACT!

Many holidays take place in winter. We celebrate New Year's Day on January 1$^{st}$. We give cards and chocolates for Valentine's Day on February 14$^{th}$.

Sometimes there is so much snow that we have a day off from school. We build a snowman. We make snow angels.

These kids have built a great-looking snowman!

## Let's Explore!

- Look at the picture. What do you see that tells you winter has arrived?

- Take a nature walk outside in winter. What clues can you find in your yard or neighborhood that say winter is here?

- In a science journal, draw pictures of what you observed. Write down some words that describe what you saw, heard, and smelled.

After playing outside, we sip hot chocolate inside, where it is cozy and warm. What is *your* favorite thing to do in winter?

# Make Frost

## What You'll Need

- Two clean, dry empty tin cans with labels removed
- Tape
- Ice cubes
- Rock salt

## Directions

**1.** Ask an adult to prepare the tin cans and put tape around the top edge of each one so you don't cut yourself.

**2.** Place ice cubes in each can.

**3.** Pour rock salt on top of the ice cubes.

**4.** Continuously stir the ice around for 2-3 minutes and watch frost form on the outside of the cans.

**5.** Place one can in the refrigerator and the other in a sunny spot. What happens?

**Think About It:** From which can did the frost melt more quickly? Why?

**Answer:** The frost melted fastest from the can placed in a sunny spot. The heat from the sun sped up the melting process.

# Glossary

**camouflage** (KA-muh-flahzh): coloring or covering that makes animals, people, and objects look like their surroundings

**frost** (frawst): ice crystals that form on cold surfaces in freezing weather

**hibernate** (HYE-bur-nayt): to sleep during winter

**icicles** (EYE-si-kuhls): hanging ice formed from dripping water that freezes

Harris County Public Library, Houston, TX

# Index

# Facts for Now

Visit this Scholastic Web site for more information on winter:
**www.factsfornow.scholastic.com**
Enter the keyword **Winter**

# About the Author

Lisa M. Herrington is a freelance writer and editor. She lives in Trumbull, Connecticut, with her husband, Ryan, and her daughter, Caroline. When the snow falls, you can find her outside sledding and making snow angels with her daughter.

[8]